S0-AEN-184

Joe Biden & Kamala Harris

-

Healing from Trump's Racism, Sexism and Bigotry and Reuniting a Divided, COVID-Ridden Nation

By Jill Donalds

Table of Contents

Disclaimer

Although the author and publisher have made every effort to ensure that the information in this book was correct at press time, the author and publisher do not assume and hereby disclaim any liability to any party for any loss, damage, or disruption caused by errors or omissions, whether such errors or omissions result from negligence, accident, or any other cause.

This book is not intended as a substitute for any type of advice.

Trump's Racism

President Trump has committed so many cases of racism, and so many varieties of racism such as institutional racism, voter- and state racism, racism towards people of color, immigrants and towards other countries and fellow politicians, we do not have time to cover all of the cases.

Let us focus on the three most racist things Trump has done lately.

Let us start with this one first.

Trump is unapologetic, defending his racist twitter tirade aimed at four Democratic congresswomen of color.

This, after he told them to "go back and help repair the completely broken and crime-infested places they came from".

Unfortunately, the only thing that should surprise anyone is that he wrote "where they came from" to prevent a sentence from ending with a preposition.

Well done, Shakespeare.

Now go back to the orifice where it came from.

Of course, it was not long before Spokes-golem Kellyanne Conway jumped to his defense by who somehow sounds even more racist than her boss.

If the president did not tell these four congresswomen to return to their alleged countries of origin, to which countries did he refer?

What is your ethnicity?

Fun fact: that's how she picks up the phone. "Go for Kellyanne, what's your ethnicity?"

A few Republicans finally spoke out against Trump, including 4 out of 197 who condemned his remarks in a vote in the House.

So, most House Republicans are very much NOT ok with racism!

Which is great news with Biden because at least he has a history of working with segregationists.

Trump has been saying racist things since at least the 70's, when he said "go back where you came from" to Black families trying to rent apartments in his buildings.

Yet many news organizations are still afraid to label his comments as "racist.

The New York Times described the latest kerfuffle by saying, "Trump Fans the Flames of a Racial Fire," which sounds more like the title of Jeff Sessions' horny Confederate fan-fiction.

Even this example from his past business dealings foretold what kind of person he really is:

The lawsuit against Trump Management Company in 1973 from the Department of Justice focused on 39 properties in New York City. The government claimed that the employees were ordered to tell African-American tenants that there were no open apartments. According to an employee quoted in court documents, the company's policy was to rent only to "Jews and executives.

The Department of Justice often used consent decrees to settle discrimination cases, and offered plaintiffs satisfaction, while defendants could avoid an admission of guilt. The reasoning: Consent decrees achieved faster results with less public resentment.

Nathaniel Jones was the general counsel of the NAACP. He later became a federal judge. John Yinger, an economist specializing in residential discrimination, served as an expert witness in a number of fair-housing cases at the time. Elyse Goldweber, an attorney at the Ministry of Justice, filed the first federal indictment against Trump Management.

How can the newspapers screw this up?

Even the Jumble had the guts to tell it like it is.

Of course, Republicans say everyone is just being too nitpicky about semantics, which is something they would never do.

Like their response to Alexandria Ocasio-Cortez calling detention facilities for what they are: concentration camps.

"We all know that AOC and this crowd are a bunch of communists, they hate Israel, they hate our own country, they're calling the guards along our border—the Border Patrol agents—concentration camp guards."

Yes, because nothing says "hate Jews" like warning people about concentration camps.

In order to prove how much these detention centers are not concentration camps, Mike Pence went... went to one of the camps where the immigrants... are concentrated.

In the second holding facility, the vice president was confronted with a much different scene.

Nearly 400 men were behind cage fences, with not even enough space to lie down.

The room was hot.

The smell was strong.

The press was withdrawn within 90 seconds after the visit.

It turns out that Pence can only maintain that level of anxious face for ninety seconds.

What a record.

Once you hit ninety-one, the whole core starts to
break up.

To be clear, these horrific border facilities
absolutely meet the definition of concentration
camps, as defined by concentration camp survivors:
"A place where people are imprisoned not because
of any crimes they committed, but simply because
of who they are."

And before you say they broke the law by entering
the country, it is not a crime to request
asylum or to be a child.

That government describes asylum not as an
internationally recognized right, but as
"a discretionary benefit."

Which is nonsense, and offensive.

You may not know they are discretionary, but they
can withdraw that right.
And they have.

Giving asylum seekers safe harbor is not a benefit, it
is law and a human right.

Not that Trump would let something as trivial as the
law stop him.

The Trump administration announcing a new rule to
make thousands of migrants now

ineligible to claim asylum.

Migrants crossing through a "safe third country" must seek asylum there first.

Yes, everything is being passed off to a "safe third country."

Not to be confused with a "safe third," which is the stranger at a bar who you and your spouse try to rope into your open marriage.

Basically, Trump is trying to unload asylum seekers onto Mexico or Guatemala.

An even though neither of these countries has agreed to the plan, neither is considered safe, and Guatemala is one of the main countries people are fleeing from.

Asking them to protect asylum seekers is like asking the burglar to protect your food.

He is not going to protect your food! Run food babies! He is going to eat you!

Fortunately, Trump's policy was challenged in court, and judges have blocked his previous efforts to restrict asylum (seekers).

Trump was not only trying to stop illegal immigration; he was also trying to stop "legal" immigrants.

As if he does not like people from certain parts of the world…. or something.

Gosh!

If only there was a word for that…

Racism, Sexism, Xenophobia and Bigotry Divided America

An incredibly sad state of affairs, and something that we never could have believed in our lifetime was to see a racist President of the United States.

Who was also a xenophobe, a sexist, a religious bigot, and a pathological liar.

But our job is to change the government and change the economy.

In such a way that it works for all of us.

For the working people of the USA.

Not just the rich.

Not just the billionaires.

We will end these raids on community after community.

We will reestablish the legal protection for the 1.8 million young people in the DACA program.

America is not, and must never be okay with putting children in cages.

Our country can never stand for grabbing children - little babies - from the arms of their mothers.

When a mom with her son or daughter is traveling 1,500 dangerous miles in order to avoid violence in Guatemala.

We must welcome them.

We have to show humanity.

We are all humans.

Before we divide into the meat of this book, here are five reforms would make the asylum system manageable again and restore a healthy border control that would not fall victim to more racism, xenophobia and bigotry:

1. Humanitarian parole: 2. Entry restrictions for Central Americans in the overdue green card lines and with family legally in the United States.

2. Sponsorship of private refugees: Allows U.S. residents and organizations to sponsor refugees from abroad as planned by the State Department in 2016.

3. Expansion of guest workers: Expansion of H-2A and H-2B seasonal worker programs to include year-round jobs for Central Americans and renunciation of the H-2B cap.

4. Legalization: Legalize illegal immigrants who do not have serious criminal convictions and allow them to be reunited with their spouses and children, thus eliminating the network for future illegal immigration.

5. Processing in the ports: Remove the cap on asylum seekers in the ports of entry, process 100 percent of their claims there, and release them with a work permit that depends on their appearance in court.

These reforms will not solve all of the problems at hand, but they will divert enough of the flow to other legal channels to make the asylum process manageable again for the U.S. authorities.

Joe Biden, the New President-Elect

Early November 2020 marks a turning point.

Joe Biden is name president-elect, who could be the most ambitious democratic president for a generation.

Before COVID 19 hit America, President Donald Trump had a 50-50 chance of being re-elected as the coronavirus pandemic ravaged America.

As America saw unrest and protests that it had not seen since the 60s, his chance has now fallen.

Before COVID 19 hit America, President Donald Trump had a 50-50 chance to be re-elected because the coronavirus pandemic hit America.

When America saw unrest and protests that it hadn't seen since the 1960s, his chance has now diminished.

What Joe has is a sort of wide appeal that makes him acceptable to the broadest possible range of voters, and one of the things that's extraordinary about him is that he has always sat directly at the center of his party and he has shifted as his party has shifted left he has shifted with it.

The ideology of a politician can be measured by the way he or she votes.

In this particular election, he or she was not one of the more progressive candidates, which eliminated many progressives.

For many other people, however, it meant that he was not radical, he was not frightening.

On the other hand, the fact that he moved as his party moved means that he was open to change.

So there's this paradox where progressives want to nominate the most progressive candidate they can, but actually there is an argument that if you want to enact progressive policies it's better to elect dull candidates who are open to change than it is to elect extremely progressive standard bearers who are going to frighten off a lot more people.

Biden's policy shows that he is open to change, but like his candidacy, it is best achieved in a non-threatening and gradual way.

Looking at health care.

Although Biden does not support Medicare's more progressive proposal for everyone, he does support a government-run health care program that people can buy into.

Now because that program is so big, it can keep premiums low.

It is going to be really attractive for people who have to buy insurance on the private market.

It could eventually lead to employers just giving their employees money to buy insurance so that could lead to the same place more or less that Medicare for all was leading.

But in a more sort of gradual, less disruptive way, there is no more consequential challenge than the on-rushing climate crisis on climate change.

Biden was lukewarm on the new green deal backed by those on the left, but he has proposed a two trillion-dollar environmental plan with huge investment in green infrastructure.

He has pledged to make America carbon-neutral by 2050, so again it is a sort of gradual plan that is no less ambitious for being graduate.

These policies set him apart from recent democratic presidents.

Bill Clinton was an extremely popular president in his time he was sort of playing on the field that Ronald Reagan had set, meaning there was a sense that people were turning away from big government.

His signature policy on welfare reform, for example.

He was extremely hard on crime and kicked a lot of people out of welfare.

We must end prosperity as a way of life and make it a way to independence and dignity.

He was not very progressive, but that was the area that was left to him.

Biden plays on a completely different field.

The Americans want the federal government to intervene, but that changes with every presidency.

They are more in favor of a big government now than at any time in the past 68 years.

This gives Biden the opportunity to be more ambitious than its predecessors.

"Yes, we can".

Obama represented change in who he was, but as a politician he's instinctively cautious and he's sort of governed really like a center-right president.

Joe Biden does not embody change, but because he is so widely acceptable to so many people, and because the democratic party has moved left and because the last four years have been so chaotic he has the space to govern much more ambitiously.

Democrats will have to control both the House and the Senate, as Biden knows well.

Thanks to nearly five decades of legislative experience in 2018, the Democrats have regained the House of Representatives, giving them a majority of 36 seats, but in the Senate, the Republicans have the majority in order.

In order to get their hands on Congress, the democrats will have to keep their majority in the house and turn over at least three seats in the Senate.

Because Joe Biden has such a great attraction to so many people, he has long coattails that enhance the image of the party.

There's nothing we can't do if we do it together. If people want to see his policies enacted they know they have to elect a democratic senate and congress to do it, yet a simple majority is no guarantee that Biden would be able to pass major legislative changes.

They could be blocked by an arcane political custom called a filibuster, but there is another way Biden could deliver change, one which many presidents have made liberal use of.

And that does not require congress to sign executive orders.

He could roll back Trump's executive orders on immigration, he can roll back the Trump administration's rollback of environmental regulations.

It's going to be tough to enact his health healthcare plans without legislation, but on immigration and environmental policy, there's a great deal he can do as president without congress climate change along with covid-19.

And the Iranian nuclear agreement is a global issue that requires a world leader.

It is in this role that Biden could have the most far-reaching political impact.

His vast foreign policy experience will give him the tools to demonstrate an ambition for true international leadership that has been missed over the past four years.

Biden served on the Senate's Foreign Affairs Committee for a long time.

He would like to see America return to its role as leader of the free world.

Many democracies around the world would like that too, and there is another way that a Biden The presidency could have an effect long after its own term of office.

At the age of 78, Biden could be the oldest president of America ever, but he has big plans that are future-proof.

The Democratic Party is a bridge because there is a whole generation of leaders.

They are the future of this country.

Whether Biden serves one term or two, there will be another generation of democratic leaders maturing under him.

He knows it.

He doesn't represent the future of the party, but he is the way for the future for the party to emerge.

Biden could be an ambitious president but ultimately that ambition will amount to nothing if he fails to win.

The Hope That Joe Biden and Kamala Harris Bring

President-elect Joe Biden, in his victory speech, called for healing and cooperation, striking an optimistic tone about the prospects for a renewed and reunited America.

"My fellow Americans, the people of this nation have spoken.

They have delivered us a clear victory. A convincing victory.

A victory for "We the People."

We have won with the most votes ever cast for a presidential ticket in the history of this nation — 74 million.

I am humbled by the trust and confidence you have placed in me.

I pledge to be a President who seeks not to divide, but to unify.

Who doesn't see Red and Blue states, but a United States.

And who will work with all my heart to win the confidence of the whole people.

For that is what America is about: The people.

And that is what our Administration will be about.

I sought this office to restore the soul of America.

To rebuild the backbone of the nation — the middle class.

To make America respected around the world again and to unite us here at home.

It is the honor of my lifetime that so many millions of Americans have voted for this vision.

And now the work of making this vision real is the task of our time.

As I said many times before, I'm Jill's husband.

I would not be here without the love and tireless support of Jill, Hunter, Ashley, all of our grandchildren and their spouses, and all our family.

They are my heart.

Jill's a mom — a military mom — and an educator.

She has dedicated her life to education, but teaching isn't just what she does — it's who she is. For America's educators, this is a great day: You're going to have one of your own in the White House, and Jill is going to make a great First Lady.

And I will be honored to be serving with a fantastic vice president — Kamala Harris — who will make history as the first woman, first Black woman, first woman of South Asian descent, and first daughter of immigrants ever elected to national office in this country.

It's long overdue, and we're reminded tonight of all those who fought so hard for so many years to make this happen. But once again, America has bent the arc of the moral universe towards justice.

Kamala, Doug — like it or not — you're family. You've become honorary Bidens and there's no way out.

To all those who volunteered, worked the polls in the middle of this pandemic, local election officials — you deserve a special thanks from this nation.

To my campaign team, and all the volunteers, to all those who gave so much of themselves to make this moment possible, I owe you everything.

And to all those who supported us: I am proud of the campaign we built and ran. I am proud of the coalition we put together, the broadest and most diverse in history.

Democrats, Republicans and Independents.

Progressives, moderates and conservatives.

Young and old.

Urban, suburban and rural.

Gay, straight, transgender.

White. Latino. Asian. Native American.

And especially for those moments when this campaign was at its lowest — the African American community stood up again for me. They always have my back, and I'll have yours.

I said from the outset I wanted a campaign that represented America, and I think we did that. Now that's what I want the administration to look like.

And to those who voted for President Trump, I understand your disappointment tonight.

I've lost a couple of elections myself.

But now, let's give each other a chance.

It's time to put away the harsh rhetoric.

To lower the temperature.

To see each other again.

To listen to each other again.

To make progress, we must stop treating our opponents as our enemy.

We are not enemies. We are Americans.

The Bible tells us that to everything there is a season — a time to build, a time to reap, a time to sow. And a time to heal.

This is the time to heal in America.

Now that the campaign is over — what is the people's will? What is our mandate?

I believe it is this: Americans have called on us to marshal the forces of decency and the forces of fairness. To marshal the forces of science and the forces of hope in the great battles of our time.

The battle to control the virus.

The battle to build prosperity.

The battle to secure your family's health care.

The battle to achieve racial justice and root out systemic racism in this country.

The battle to save the climate.

The battle to restore decency, defend democracy, and give everybody in this country a fair shot.

Our work begins with getting COVID under control.

We cannot repair the economy, restore our vitality, or relish life's most precious moments — hugging a grandchild, birthdays, weddings, graduations, all the moments that matter most to us — until we get this virus under control.

On Monday, I will name a group of leading scientists and experts as Transition Advisors to help take the Biden-Harris COVID plan and convert it into an action blueprint that starts on January 20th, 2021.

That plan will be built on a bedrock of science. It will be constructed out of compassion, empathy, and concern.

I will spare no effort — or commitment — to turn this pandemic around.

I ran as a proud Democrat. I will now be an American president. I will work as hard for those who didn't vote for me — as those who did.

Let this grim era of demonization in America begin to end — here and now.

The refusal of Democrats and Republicans to cooperate with one another is not due to some mysterious force beyond our control.

It's a decision. It's a choice we make.

And if we can decide not to cooperate, then we can decide to cooperate. And I believe that this is part of the mandate from the American people. They want us to cooperate.

That's the choice I'll make. And I call on the Congress — Democrats and Republicans alike — to make that choice with me.

The American story is about the slow, yet steady widening of opportunity.

Make no mistake: Too many dreams have been deferred for too long.

We must make the promise of the country real for everybody — no matter their race, their ethnicity, their faith, their identity, or their disability.

America has always been shaped by inflection points — by moments in time where we've made hard decisions about who we are and what we want to be.

Lincoln in 1860 — coming to save the Union.

FDR in 1932 — promising a beleaguered country a New Deal.

JFK in 1960 — pledging a New Frontier.

And twelve years ago — when Barack Obama made history — and told us, "Yes, we can."

We stand again at an inflection point.

We have the opportunity to defeat despair and to build a nation of prosperity and purpose.

We can do it. I know we can.

I've long talked about the battle for the soul of America.

We must restore the soul of America.

Our nation is shaped by the constant battle between our better angels and our darkest impulses.

It is time for our better angels to prevail.

Tonight, the whole world is watching America. I believe at our best America is a beacon for the globe.

And we lead not by the example of our power, but by the power of our example.

I've always believed we can define America in one word: Possibilities.

That in America everyone should be given the opportunity to go as far as their dreams and God-given ability will take them.

You see, I believe in the possibility of this country.

We're always looking ahead.

Ahead to an America that's freer and more just.

Ahead to an America that creates jobs with dignity and respect.

Ahead to an America that cures disease — like cancer and Alzheimer's.

Ahead to an America that never leaves anyone behind.

Ahead to an America that never gives up, never gives in.

This is a great nation.

And we are a good people.

This is the United States of America.

And there has never been anything we haven't been able to do when we've done it together.

In the last days of the campaign, I've been thinking about a hymn that means a lot to me and to my family, particularly my deceased son Beau. It captures the faith that sustains me and which I believe sustains America.

And I hope it can provide some comfort and solace to the more than 230,000 families who have lost a loved one to this terrible virus this year. My heart goes out to each and every one of you. Hopefully this hymn gives you solace as well.

"And He will raise you up on eagle's wings,

Bear you on the breath of dawn,

Make you to shine like the sun,

And hold you in the palm of His Hand."

And now, together — on eagle's wings — we embark on the work that God and history have called upon us to do.

With full hearts and steady hands, with faith in America and in each other, with a love of country — and a thirst for justice — let us be the nation that we know we can be.

A nation united.

A nation strengthened.

A nation healed.

The United States of America.

God bless you.

And may God protect our troops. 'A new day of hope for America'

Parts of the nation erupted in celebration as the news was called and scenes of cheering and singing flooded social media Saturday. Biden's apparent win is historic because he broke Barack Obama's record for most votes cast for a U.S. presidential candidate, and also because it means Sen. Kamala Harris is set to become the first female vice president and woman of color in the White House.

"I am honored and humbled by the trust the American people have placed in me and in Vice President-elect Harris," Biden said in a statement after major media outlets projected him as the winner. "In the face of unprecedented obstacles, a record number of Americans voted. Proving once again, that democracy beats deep in the heart of America."

"With the campaign over, it's time to put the anger and the harsh rhetoric behind us and come together as a nation," the statement added. "It's time for America to unite. And to heal. We are the United States of America. And there's nothing we can't do, if we do it together."

We want a country that is not broken by racism and bigotry,

We want leadership that can create opportunities for all Americans to succeed in all aspects of society, without fear of over-policing, discrimination, and destructive policies at our expense.

Former President Barack Obama said he "could not be prouder" to congratulate Biden and Harris.

Speaker of the House Nancy Pelosi added that their victory "marks the dawning of a new day of hope for America.

After the darkness, division and hate of the past four years, America has spoken and rejected more of the same.

'Welcome back': The allies of the USA celebrate the Biden win and hope for a U.S. return to the global stage of politics."

Joe Biden: Plans for "Made In America"

Joe Biden will get busy for the next four years. Below is an overview of the most important policy changes he would like to implement as soon as he moves into the White House in January.

First of all, a disclaimer: Biden's ability to realize his plans often depends on the room for maneuver he will soon have in the House of Representatives and the Senate, i.e. the U.S. Lower and U.S. Senate. Chances are that the Democrats at Biden's inauguration will have a majority in the House, but not in the Senate.

1. Getting the coronavirus under control

Biden mentioned earlier that he considers getting the coronavirus under control as one of his most important tasks.

For example, he wants to insist on wearing mouth caps all over the country. He also wants to appoint a group of experts who will be responsible for producing coronate tests. He also promised to make coronate tests, treatments and vaccines free of charge for all Americans.

2. Stimulating domestic production

In order for the U.S. to recover from the corona concession, the newly elected president wants to force government agencies to buy goods and services of U.S. manufacture, in order to stimulate domestic production.

Biden also wants to undo some of the tax cuts that President Trump has introduced that will benefit large corporations and wealthy Americans. In addition, Biden promises to strengthen trade union rights soon after his inauguration.

3. An anti-discrimination law for the LGBTQ+ community and more gender equality

In the first hundred days of his term of office, Biden wants to ensure that the so-called Equality Act is passed. This act has to protect people against discrimination based on sexuality and gender.

In addition, Biden wants to set up a council for gender equality in the White House to ensure that the policies of the federal government take women into account.

4. Guarantee 11 million immigrants U.S. citizenship and reverse Trumps policies

On the first day of his term of office, Biden wants to send a bill to the U.S. Congress that includes a procedure to guarantee U.S. citizenship to 11 million illegal immigrants.

Furthermore, Biden wants to reverse as much as possible the measures taken by President Trump in the field of immigration. Among other things, he wants to lift the travel ban on travelers from thirteen countries, mainly Islamic or African countries. He also hopes to reunite more than five hundred children with their families, who became separated at the border with Mexico under the Trump government.

5. Restoring international relations and regaining the trust of allies

Biden will have to restore many international relations after President Trump's America First policy. Biden promises to call American allies on the first day of his presidency in an effort to regain their trust.

One of Biden's other plans before the start of his term of office is to reverse President Trump's controversial decision to leave the World Health Organization (WHO). Biden also wants to rejoin the Paris Climate Accord, where Trump stepped down during his term of office.

Biden would also like to let Moscow know as soon as possible that he is willing to extend the last American-Russian treaty on nuclear weapons. That treaty expires sixteen days after Biden's inauguration.

Furthermore, Biden wants to consult the most important allies before he decides on his policy regarding relations with Beijing and the establishment of American tariffs on Chinese products.

6. Tackling climate pollutants and striving for a completely clean economy in 2050

In addition to joining the Paris Climate Accord, Biden hopes to restore the Obama administration's climate policy. For example, he wants to reduce the use of coal and gas and reduce methane emissions from oil and gas production.

Furthermore, he announced his intention to build a special climate department in the U.S. Department of Justice that will actively enforce the policy on polluters. In the long term, Passenger's climate policy must be the start of the pursuit of a completely clean economy in 2050.

How Biden Will Reunite a Broken Nation and the World

Uncle Sam is back with a Joe Biden presidency, the big buddy to the rest of the world that had its back, for the greater global good.

Well yes, but it is also quite different this time. After four years of isolationist policies and an estrangement from global bodies like the World Health Organization and NATO, Biden will patch things back together.

Under a Biden Presidency, the United States will move from a "with or without us" approach to a policy that believes and stands for principles that the US can achieve more if we work together with other countries.

A White House without a Trump should bring a less racist world.

Biden will repair fences with allies and partners, his focus is on repairing all the deep divisions within American society that Trump will leave behind.

Before even announcing his cabinet or his White House team, Biden will form a national COVID-19 task force to combat the alarming surge in cases as numbers broke through 100,000 a day.

On the task force's agenda will be the distribution of the coronavirus vaccine, a federal standard for mask protocols and funding for hospitals and healthcare under the supervision of the state that has jumped under successive virus waves.

Joe Biden will also rejoin the Paris Agreement on Climate Change that Trump dumped in mid-2017, but without control of the Senate will find it hard to put in effect his green energy plan. Biden will do his absolute best to reduce reliance on fossil fuels, with the goal to make emissions cleaner.

Within the United States, Americans can expect Biden to roll back Trump orders on immigration and instead focus on human rights issues with Latin neighbors.

But what will happen to the wall being built on the US southern border to stop the flow of illegal immigration?

Joe Biden has pledged that there will not be another foot of wall constructed under his administration, but that does not start until his January 20 inauguration.

The new president intends to instead focus on security issues with the border, most importantly stopping the traffic of illegal drugs and other contraband into the US.

Despite political roadblocks for his domestic priorities, Biden's power to shape US foreign policy will be considerable.

Back at it!

The relationship of China and the United States of America has plunged amid disputes over trade, technology, human rights, and the origins of the coronavirus and its aftermath: a worldwide pandemic.

Biden is not expected to abolish all imposed tariffs, but it is expected to abolish agricultural tariffs in exchange for something from the Chinese government.

In his first hundred days in office, Biden will do more than Trump did four years earlier, and this will almost certainly include an investigating whether Russia has interfered with the elections.

Joe's Pandemic Plan

Joe Biden has a critical task ahead of him: containing COVID-19. Biden has reportedly already started working on the transition of power with his team, including coordinating his strategy for COVID-19.

As the world awaits the first vaccine and coronavirus infections surge, Biden has acknowledged that the pandemic will not end anytime soon, but he has said he will rely on the counsel of scientists and medical professionals.

It will take a lot of hard work to end this pandemic

Joe promises this: We will start on Day 1 doing the right things.

While the U.S. makes up approximately 4% of the world's population, it has had approximately 20% of all COVID-19 cases.

That makes you think.

The U.S. daily total of coronavirus infections rose by approximately 130,000 in November, a fourth straight day of record-setting levels, as hospitals in rural areas of the Midwest and southern states including Texas and Florida continued to feel the strain.

The Infectious Diseases Society of America told MarketWatch that Biden's plans for combating the pandemic reflects its own key tenets.

Since the pandemic began, IDSA has called for a comprehensive and well-coordinated response rooted in the best available scientific data.

Clear communication with the public is an essential component of efforts to control the pandemic. Collecting and sharing data in a transparent manner is important to build public trust and to help people make informed decisions to reduce their risk of transmission

While the scientific community has traditionally stayed out of politics, the medical journal Nature endorsed Biden's bid for the presidency and his pandemic plan.

Biden has shown that he respects the values of research and has vowed to work to restore the United States' fractured global relationships. For these reasons, Nature is endorsing Biden.

Biden's campaign has worked closely with researchers to develop comprehensive plans on COVID-19 and climate change. He has pledged that decisions on the pandemic response will be made by public-health professionals and not by politicians.

Biden is also rightly committing to restoring the ability of these professionals to communicate directly with the public.

Biden has pledged to put "scientists and public-health leaders front and center" to communicate with the American public and to ensure the federal government has primary responsibility on the coronavirus.

A summary of Biden's pandemic plan

1. Push for a national mask mandate.

While on the campaign trail, Biden vowed to push for more Americans to wear masks. He said "First, I'll go to every governor and urge them to mandate mask wearing in their states, and, if they refuse, I'll go to the mayors and county executives and get local mask requirements in place nationwide."

Trump always used to refer to mask wearing as "politically correct."

Further, modeling suggests that near universal masking could prevent 180,000 COVID-19 deaths. We continue to support a national mask mandate.

2. Paid sick leave and caregiving leave

In addition to his pledge to raise the federal minimum wage to $15 an hour from $7.25 an hour, Biden has said the pandemic has highlighted the lack of labor protections for millions of workers, such as paid sick and caregiving leave, and he advocates hazard pay, for essential workers who risk their health and are typically paid low wages.

President-elect Biden's goal of strengthening the workforce needed to respond to COVID-19 and prepare for future pandemics is laudable, and this workforce must include public health professionals, clinicians and scientists, as approximately 208 million Americans live in areas with little or no access to an infectious diseases physician.

3. CDC tracker for coronavirus patients

Earlier this year, the U.S. Department of Health and Human Services temporarily changed the way hospitals reported critical information on the coronavirus pandemic to the government, taking the responsibility for data collection away from the Centers for Disease Control and Prevention. After a backlash from public-health officials, however, the department reversed that decision in August.

Biden said wants more transparency. He said he will instruct the CDC to establish real-time dashboards tracking hospital admissions related to COVID-19, especially for ICUs and emergency departments, in concert with the American Hospital Association and large hospital chains and supply-chain information on personal protective equipment and other important supplies.

4. Protecting and restoring Obamacare

Protecting Obamacare will be one of the first priorities for President Biden. He previously expressed fears that a U.S. Supreme Court conservative 6-3 majority, made possible by newly confirmed Justice Amy Coney Barrett, could finally dismantle former President Barack Obama's Affordable Care Act, and deprive millions of people of health-care coverage.

Some 7.7 million Americans who were laid off during the pandemic lost their employer-sponsored health coverage as of June. Those plans covered some 6.9 million of their dependents, impacting up to 14.6 million individuals, according to a report published by the Commonwealth Fund, a private foundation that supports health-care issues.5. Free COVID-19 tests for all

Biden has pledged free testing for all Americans, whether or not they have health insurance: that is, no co-payments, no deductibles, and no surprise medical billing. "We should be investigating a great deal more money in testing and tracing," he told CBS News this month. "It's not enough to know in seven days or five days or three days whether or not you have COVID."

IDSA agrees with increasing access to testing and testing capacity. In addition to ensuring that everyone who needs a test can get one, we must also improve turnaround time on tests to ensure results are sufficiently rapid to effectively inform contact tracing, isolation, and quarantine. We also need a strategy to ensure a sufficient inventory of tests and testing supplies.

We created this rush, and we did not have the ability to test or quarantine those people, so that seeded the disease here.

Dr. Anthony Fauci, an immunologist and the director of the National Institute of Allergy and Infectious Diseases and an expert in infectious diseases for the last four decades, has expressed concerns about a "twindemic" of COVID-19 and seasonal influenza as the U.S. enters flu season, and urged Americans to get their flu shots.

Fauci remains hopeful that a coronavirus vaccine could be developed by early 2021 but has repeatedly said it's unlikely that a vaccine will deliver 100%

immunity. He said the best realistic outcome, based on other vaccines, would be 70% to 75% effective. The measles vaccine, he said, is among the most effective by providing 97% immunity.

Returning to a life beyond COVID-19 will not happen until the end of 2021. But it will probably be enough to begin opening colleges and universities, and schools. That too will depend on any vaccine, its distribution, and its effectiveness.

Companies are currently working on vaccines. We never had an efficient testing regime so we could quickly identify people, isolate them, and prevent spread. We did not have effective implementation uniformly across the country, with the public health measures: physical distancing, facemask wearing, limiting crowds is critical to that.

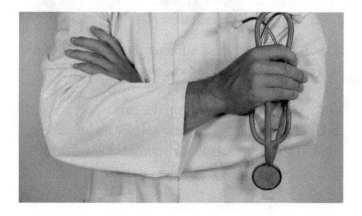

Pfizer Announces 'A Breakthrough'

Early November 2020, Pharmaceutical company Pfizer announces a Corona vaccine 90 percent effective and safe.

Pfizer seems to be the first to come up with a vaccine against corona. A market demand follows at the end of this month, reports the U.S. pharmacist. Pfizer's latest research results, published today, show that the vaccine has a tremendous success rate. Experts react enthusiastically, but still see a catch.

These are the first results of Phase 3 research, the final stage before a vaccine can enter the market. In that phase, the vaccine was tested on more than 43,000 people. A first analysis shows that 94 subjects received the coronavirus. The vast majority were in the placebo group, reports Pfizer, which concludes that based on the numbers, the vaccine appears to be 90 percent effective.

That percentage is much higher than expected and then is necessary to market a vaccine. In comparison, most vaccines have an effectiveness rate of around 80 percent; in the case of corona, health authorities are already satisfied with an effectiveness rate of over 50 percent.

Side effects

For the time being, there have not been any major problems with side effects during the studies of the vaccine, reports the American pharmacist.

Although not all the results are in yet, Pfizer Director Albert Bourla speaks of a "huge breakthrough. With this news, we are a significant step closer to a vaccine that will put an end to this global health crisis.

But there is still a catch. The question remains to what extent the vaccine is effective in the longer term. These results do not yet allow us to say that.

The high effectiveness of over 90 percent might not last. It might decline somewhat in the long term.

Time will tell.

Joe Biden's Economic Plan: Save the Middle Class to Save America

It is fair to say that Joe Biden's eligibility has been more discussed than his policy. The former vice president is defined by what he is not - radical or revolutionary.

Joe Biden is seen by many Democrats as the most suitable candidate to challenge President Trump in today's deeply polarized political landscape.

And now he is the new elect president!

Biden received a lot of support as soon as he announced that he would be running for the third time in his career.

The 77-year-old's economic agenda is not as detailed as others and does not include similar sweeping proposals, but his plan for the U.S. is still ambitious and represents more than a reassuring reset button for Americans rattled by Trump.

The Middle Class in America

Revitalizing the middle class and making it more racist is the cornerstone of Biden's campaign. "This country was not built by Wall Street bankers and CEOs and hedge fund managers.

America was built by the American middle class.

Biden does not think 500 billionaires are the reason we are in trouble. The people at the top are not bad guys.

But he does believe that a growing and thriving middle class, which he thinks about more in terms of values and lifestyle than an income group, is important for social and political stability in the U.S. He blames the lack of opportunity and optimism in the country for "fake populism" and "a younger generation questioning the essence of our capitalist system.

According to Pew Research, 52% of American adults lived in middle-income households in 2016. These are adults with an annual income of two-thirds to double the national median, after incomes have been adjusted to the size of the household.

The annual income range for a middle-class household of three in 2016 was $45,200 to $135,600.

The U.S. has a proportionately smaller middle class than many advanced economies, and income disparities among middle class groups are increasing. While the top 20% has fully recovered from the Great Recession, it looks like the middle class has not yet reached its previous peak in 2007.

Biden had this to say: "People in the middle class are in trouble. It is not just their perception. They're in trouble."

Biden's Healthcare Plan

Official data say the uninsured rate rose to 8.5% of the U.S. population for the first time since 2008-2009 from 7.9% in 2018 to 8.5% in 2017, and Biden blamed the numerous trump card policy attacks on the Affordable Care Act.

As our new president, he pledges to protect and build on the ACA. Though he wants to insure health care is a right for all and not a privilege, he does not support Health Care for All and eliminating private insurance because it would mean getting rid of the hard-won Obamacare and starting over on political negotiations. He also argued during the September 12 debate that Medicare for All would cost more than $30 trillion over 10 years.

Biden promises his Obamacare healthcare proposal will expand to insure 97% of Americans and cost $750 billion over 10 years. He wants to introduce a public health insurance option such as Medicare that will be available on a premium-free basis to individuals in states that have not expanded

Medicaid and people who make under 138% of the federal poverty level.

Joe Biden also wants to eliminate the 400% of federal poverty-level income cap for tax credit eligibility and lower-employee maximum contribution coverage of up to 8.5%.

In addition to this, he pledged to bar healthcare providers from "surprise billing" patients with out-of-network rates, address market concentration in the industry, allow Medicare to negotiate lower prices with drug manufacturers, establish an independent review committee that will recommend a reasonable price for uncompetitive drugs, punish drug price increases over the inflation rate, end the tax deduction for all prescription drug advertising, support the development of generic drugs and restore federal funding for planned parenthood.

Biden also promised to fight for reducing the Medicare eligibility age to 60 from 65. "It points to the reality that, even after the current crisis ends, older Americans are likely to find it difficult to secure jobs," he spoke.

Biden wants additional costs to be funded from general revenues to protect the Medicare Trust Fund.

Biden's Tax Plan

Biden wants a pro-growth, progressive tax law. His plan is to generate nearly $4 trillion in additional revenue in a decade. According to the Center for Tax Policy, "the highest-income 20% of households (which will make about $170,000 or more) would bear nearly 93% of the burden of Biden's proposed tax increase, and the highest 1% almost three quarters.

Here are the changes Biden wants to make:

- Raise the top income tax rate back to 39.6% from 37%
- Tax capital gains and dividends at standard rates for people with an annual income of more than $1 million
- Tax unrealized capital gains on death
- Applying social security payroll tax for those earning more than $400,000 a year
- Increase of the highest corporate income tax rate from 21% to 28%
- 15% minimum tax rate on the accounting income of large enterprises (at least 100 million U.S. dollars net annual income)
- Tax profits of foreign subsidiaries of U.S. companies 21%

Student Debt

After Bernie Sanders suspended his run, Biden expanded his student debt plan and said that he wants to forgive all education-related federal student debt of those who make up $125,000 and attended public universities and two- and four-year colleges, historic black colleges and universities and under-funded minority service institutions.

Biden says he will finance this by withdrawing the high-income "excess business losses" tax cut in the CARES code. "That tax cut will overwhelmingly benefit the richest Americans and is unnecessary for tackling the current COVID-19 economic aid effort."

He has several other federal student debt proposals including, immediately canceling a minimum of $10,000 of student debt per person (Sen. Elizabeth Warren's idea), forgiving the rest of loans after 20 years without a tax charge, suspending monthly payments and interest from those earning less than $25,000 a year and capping payments at 5% of discretionary income for the remainder, and additional federal loan forgiveness of up to $50,000 over five years for those participating in the public service.

Biden has also adapted to Sanders' plan to free up public colleges and universities for everyone, regardless of income, and has only applied it to families with an income of less than $125,000.

Biden has basically fully supported and approved Warren's plan to change the personal bankruptcy laws he helped shape. With the title "Fixing Our Bankruptcy System to Give People a Second Chance," it makes student loans losable. Streamlining and simplifying the bankruptcy filing process to make it cheaper and more flexible is the proposal.

Workers' Rights

Biden supports raising the federal minimum wage to $15. Our new president also wants to give employees more bargaining power by getting rid of "abusive" non-competition clauses, starting with removing certain rules in contracts that prevent employees from talking about wages, and by discouraging companies from classifying low-wage workers as managers to avoid paying overtime.

Joe Biden also wants international trade rules that "protect our employees, protect the environment, enforce labor standards and middle-class wages, promote innovation and address major global challenges such as business concentration, corruption and last but not least, climate change.

Infrastructure

As vice president, Biden once called New York's LaGuardia a third-world airport in a U.S. infrastructure speech: "Look, we need roads, we need waterways, we need ports to move our products. We need highways and transit to get employees to and from work. We need lightning fast broadband to communicate.

Infrastructure is not a luxury. It is an absolute necessity to compete with the rest of the world. We need a huge investment in infrastructure: roads, bridges, airports, broadband. We are too many years behind, and we can afford it.

Biden plans to spend $1.3 trillion on infrastructure over a decade. This includes $50 billion in his first year in office on repairing roads, highways and bridges, $20 billion on rural broadband infrastructure, $400 billion more than 10 years on a federal new agency to conduct clean energy research and innovation, $5 billion more than five years on electric car battery technology and $10 billion more than 10 years on transit projects serving areas of high poverty.

Rural America

Biden wants to help rural communities, which make up 20% of the U.S. population, by fighting for fair trade agreements, invest $20 billion in rural broadband infrastructure, create low-carbon production jobs, reinvest in agricultural research, improve access to federal funds and funds for agriculture or small businesses, expand health services and medical training programs, and spend 10% of federal programs on areas of persistent poverty.

The Vital Role of Kamal Harris

Kamala Harris enjoyed the moment when she became the first woman, and the first Black and Asian American, who became vice president, with a very warm smile.

Just over a year ago, when the Senator from California was hoping to win the Democratic nomination for president, she launched a powerful attack on Joe Biden during a debate about the race. Many thought it was a heavy blow to his ambitions. But by the end of the year, her campaign was dead, and it was Mr. Biden who returned the 56-year-old to the national spotlight by putting her on his ticket.

The first female, first Black and first South Asian vice-president, represents a new face of political power after an election about who has the power and how they use it.

"It's a big reversal of fortune for Kamala Harris," said Gil Duran, a communications director for Ms. Harris in 2013, who criticized her for the presidential nomination. "Many people thought she didn't have the discipline and focus to move up to a position in the White House so quickly.... although people knew she had ambition and star potential. It was always clear that she had the raw talent."

Who is Kamala Harris?

Born in Oakland, California, to two immigrant parents. Her mother is Indian and her father Jamaican. Her parents divorced when she was five years old and she was raised mainly by her Hindu single mother, Shyamala Gopalan Harris, a cancer researcher and previously a dedicated civil rights activist.

Kamala grew up with her Indian ancestry and visited India with her mother, but Mrs. Harris has said that her mother adopted the Black culture of Oakland and immersed her two daughters - Kamala and her younger sister Maya.

Her mother understood very well that she was raising two Black daughters. "She knew that her adopted homeland would see Maya and me as Black girls and she was determined that we would grow into confident, proud Black women," she wrote in The Truths We Hold - her autobiography.

Because of her biracial roots and upbringing, she embodies and can appeal to many American identities. Those parts of the country that have seen rapid demographic change, enough change to change the politics of a region, see an ambitious symbol in her.

But it was her time at Howard University, one of the country's leading historical black colleges and universities, that she has described as one of the most formative experiences of her life.

Lita Rosario-Richardson met Kamala Harris when she met in the 1980s in Howard in the Yard area of the campus to talk about politics, fashion, and gossip.

They had a connection to the campus Republicans, their experience with single mothers, even though they are both the scales. It was also a politically shaping era.

Reagan was president at the time, and it was the apartheid era and there was a lot of talk about rejection with 'trans Africa' and the Martin Luther King vacation issue. We know that as descendants of enslaved people and people of color from colonization, we have a special role and that having an education gives us a special position in society to help bring about change," says Rosario-Richardson.

It was a philosophy and a call to action that was part of the university experience of Ms. Harris', who returned to address Howard's students in 2017 and took them on a journey from the Ferguson protests of 2014 to the halls of Capitol Hill in one sentence:

"Your students joined the fight for justice - you protested. From the streets of Ferguson to the halls of the U.S. Congress, you have lived the words of James Baldwin: "There is never a time in the future when we will work out our salvation. The challenge is in the moment, time is always now".

Kamala Harris also operates with ease in predominantly white communities. Her early years included a short period in Canada. However, Harris says she has always felt comfortable with her identity and simply describes herself as "American".

She told the Washington Post in 2019 that politicians should not fit in boxes because of their color or background.

In 2014, Senator Harris married attorney Doug Emhoff - now a regular at her campaign stops - and became stepmother to his two children.

Last year she wrote an article for Elle magazine about the experience of becoming a stepmother and revealed the name that would come to dominate many headlines that followed.

"When Doug and I got married, Cole, Ella and I agreed that we didn't like the term 'stepmother'. Instead, they came up with the name 'Momala'.

They were portrayed as the embodiment of the modern American "blended" family, an image that the media took to and one that occupied many column inches about how we talk about female politicians.

If she becomes vice-president, she probably won't lose this nickname, but many claim that she should also be seen and recognized as the descendant of another kind of family and that is the heir of generations of Black female activists.

"She is heir to a legacy of the people's organizers, elected officials, and unsuccessful candidates who paved the way to the White House. Black women are seen as a political force of nature in democratic politics and the Democratic Party," said Nadia Brown, university lecturer in political science and African-American studies at Purdue University, at the BBC.

Fannie Lou Hamer, Ella Baker and Septima Clark are some of the names that they follow in the footsteps of, Ms. Hamer.

The victory of Kamala Harris is historic, but it is not hers. It is shared with countless Black women who made this day possible.

A Witty Debater

But from the very first moment, as her friend, Mrs. Rosario-Richardson, testifies, she showed the skills that enabled her to be one of the few women to break through the barriers.

That is what attracted her to become a member of the debate team at Howard University. Wittiness and humor are part of that arsenal. The smile with which she greeted the president-elect, as she made that first memorable phone call, was one that immediately and intimately recognized her friend.

That clearly shows the personality of Kamal Harris, even in the short time she was on the campaign trail. She's always laughed, she's always had a sense of humor - even in the context of a university debate - to get those points across.

The ability to deliver singers to her opponents in the live debate was part of the momentum behind the beginning of her bid for the Democratic presidential nomination. She was not afraid of the confrontation.

"Why is @KamalaHarris the only person who laughs at her jokes... always far too long and far too loud?" Mr. Trump's son tweeted.

"You wouldn't know a joke if they raised you," she tweeted back.

A harmless social media burn, but a popular shorthand for the kind of skills that meant a career in law and politics was a natural fit.

Between Left and Right

Although her career as a public prosecutor made her a politician, it brought political benefits and risks.

She began working in the Alameda County District Attorney's Office and became the district attorney - the top prosecutor - for San Francisco in 2003, before being elected the first woman and the first Black person to serve as California's Attorney General, the top attorney and law enforcement officer in the most populous state of America.

Kamal gained a reputation as one of the rising stars of the Democratic Party and used this momentum to drive her election as California's junior U.S. Senator in 2017.

But the line between pleasing left-handed California Democrats and being a politician for a nation where the left does not decide who becomes president has been difficult.

She gained favor among progressives for her acerbic questioning when the Supreme Court appointed

Brett Kavanaugh. But some say that by walking the thin line between her party's progressive and moderate wings, she ultimately appealed to neither.

Despite a left-wing attitude towards issues such as same-sex marriage and the death penalty, she faced repeated attacks because she was not really progressive enough.

"Kamala is a cop" became a common chorus on the campaign trail. Maybe true, but those same credentials of law enforcement proved beneficial at the national stage when Democrats had to persuade more moderate voters and independents.

She was "someone with a law enforcement background and was seen in her own state as insufficiently progressive... and tried to project an inauthentic self. That looks quite different in a vice-presidential slot" said Mr. Duran.

While the U.S. is struggling with ongoing racial reckoning and police brutality is being monitored, Kamala Harris has been sitting in the front row, using her large microphone.

On talk shows she calls for changes in U.S. police practices, on Twitter she calls for the arrest of the police officers who murdered Breonna Taylor, a 26-year-old Kentucky African-American woman, and she often talks about the need to dismantle systemic racism.

She has a background in law enforcement, but she has often said that her identity makes her uniquely qualified to represent marginalized people.

Now she gets the opportunity to do so.

As an insider in the White House.

Kamala Harris as our new vice-president

The history of the Senator of California winning also represents the millions of women in demographics -- often overlooked, historically under-represented and systematically ignored -- who are now the recipients of that new power for the first time in the country's 200-plus-year history.

Harris and Biden's victory comes days after a lengthy vote count that reflects a deeply divided electorate. It symbolizes book support for the Trump era, which followed the first Black U.S. president and was carried by social wrongs, including white domination.

Harris' triumph marks a new culmination in a career of barrier-breaking achievements, from San Francisco's district attorney to California's attorney general and the U.S.'s second-largest Black senator.

Her presence testifies the dedication of generations before Meher.

Harris said in her first speech as elected vice president: "Women and men who believed so strongly in the promise of equality, freedom and justice for all."

She Will Not Be the Last

While Kamala Harris may be the first woman in this office, she will not be the last!

"Because every little girl watching tonight sees that this is a land of opportunity, and to the children of our country, regardless of your gender, our country has sent you a clear message: Dream with ambition, lead with conviction, and see yourself in a way that others may not see, simply because they have never seen it before. But know that we will applaud you every step of the way," says Harris.

Harris went to Howard University, a historic Black university in Washington. Her time at Howard, where she joined Alpha Kappa Alpha Sorority Inc., profoundly shaped her political vision.

You did not have to let someone else's idea of what it means to be Black restrict you. "You could be a fine art student as well as a class president. You could be homecoming queen and the head of the science club. You could be a member of a student union and be in government and want to go to law school, and it would encourage you to be yourself.

As a Black and South Asian woman in an overwhelming white arena, Harris was a kind of pioneer on her trip to the White House. And the voters noticed. It just feels like Black girls like Harris can run for class president, Black girls like Kamal can go for the big things in life.

An aspiring Senator in the U.S. herself, Shadrach told Harris at the end of her ambition to chart a path like Harris'. According to Shadrach, Harris said that "as long as I think about it and do my best to be the best version of me, I will be able to achieve my goals".

Harris won the Democratic presidential ticket, a very big step for girls and women who look like her. She was the one who could prove that it is really possible. You see some kind of connection because we are two similar people. Many can identify with her.

Harris is a lot of things outside of her gender and her race, of course. But her presence alone brings so much - so much for those, of all ages, who see themselves in her.

Harris is not shy to emphasize her upbringing or her influences, as was clear from her shouting at AKA's and HBCU's during her DNC speech.

Harris loves the nickname for America's nine historic Black Brotherhoods and Student Clubs and nods to the fact that she was the first graduate of an historic Black college or university to be selected as the candidate of a major party.

Harris' remarks could no longer contrast with the rhetoric of President Donald Trump over the past four years.

While Trump spent his tenure in the White House excelling at being different and supporting the country's many hierarchies, Harris used the campaign process to do exactly the opposite.

Harris' bid was a pure distillation of the complex joy of representation. Often in her Converse sneakers, the former prosecutor made space for women of color to tell their lived experiences during campaign events on the trail.

She made a point to prop up women of color small business owners, frequently telling them to say their companies' names clearly in front of the press so they could be included in news stories.

Certain voters felt, in today's parlance, seen. And come Inauguration Day, that visibility will extend to the White House and, likely, alchemize into substantive representation.

There is a sobering result of Harris' historic victory. Her success says as much about America's political institutions as it does about her.

Kamala Harris is the first female, the first Black and the first South Asian vice president-elect is both an affirmation of her excellence -- her skill as a debater against Mike Pence, for example -- and a reflection of the racism and sexism that punishes women of color running for executive office.

And while it is true that Harris achieved even more firsts this week, it's perhaps more accurate to describe these firsts as only.

Kamala Harris is the only female, only Black and only South Asian vice president elected.

So far.

Harris' mother said it best: "Kamala, you may be the first to do many things, but make sure you're not the last."

Why Overcoming Racism and Differences is Essential

Respectful and tolerant societies are typically the most harmonious. To get through the many difficult challenges of the 21st Century, we need to learn to overcome racism and bigotry.

Humans are the most cooperative species on the planet – all part of a huge, interconnected ecosystem. We have managed to build vast cities, connected by a global nervous system of roads, shipping lanes, optical fibers, and whatnot.

We have sent many satellites spinning around the planet. Even seemingly simple objects like a graphite pencil are the work of thousands of hands from around the world, as the wonderful essay I-Pencil, describes.

"I, Pencil, simple though I appear to be, merit your wonder and awe ... if you can become aware of the miraculousness which I symbolize, you can help save the freedom mankind is so unhappily losing. I have a profound lesson to teach. And I can teach this lesson better than can an automobile or an airplane or a mechanical dishwasher because — well, because I am seemingly so simple.

Simple?

Yet not a single person on the face of this Earth knows how to make me.

Yet we can also be surprisingly intolerant of each other. If we are completely honest, there is perhaps a little bit of xenophobia, racism, sexism, and bigotry deep within all of us.

Luckily, we can choose to control and suppress such tendencies for our own wellbeing and also, for the good of our shared society.

Most human attitudes and behavior have both a genetic and an environmental component. This is also true for our fear of others who are different to us – xenophobia – and intolerance of their viewpoints – bigotry. Hardwired into the brain's amygdala region is a fear reflex that is primed by encounters with the unfamiliar.

In early dawn of human civilization, it made sense to be fearful of other groups. They could have been violent, steal resources, or introduce new diseases we are not adapted to. Conversely, it was beneficial to trust those who look similar to us – they were more likely to be related.

When we helped these kin, our own genes were more likely to be passed to future generations. What is more, if the other persons reciprocated the good deeds, we would all benefit (a lot!) more.

Apart from genetic influences, our human culture strongly influences our attitudes and behavior, modifying our human drives, which either suppressing them or encouraging them further.

Whether we tolerate and trust someone or fear and reject them depends a lot on this culture.

Modern civilization in general encourages the extension of attitudes such as respect and tolerance beyond those who look similar to us, to those who we have no relation to.

We reinforce and codify these values, teaching them to our children, while some religious and secular spiritual leaders promote them in their teachings.

This because doing so generally lead to a more harmonious, mutually beneficial society, and that is exactly what has made us such a cooperative species.

But sometimes our cultures can be less progressive. Whether we like it or not; wat people around us say and do subconsciously influences the way we think.

We soak up this cultural context like a sponge, and it subtly shapes our attitudes and behaviors. If we are surrounded by people that stigmatize those different to themselves, this also encourages distrust or aggression in us. Making us worse than we could be.

It presses the buttons of certain deep-seated xenophobic attitudes within us. In fact, it discourages the hard-learned inhibitory responses in the brain's prefrontal cortex that get built up under more progressive contexts.

A healthy pride in one's country can easily tip into unhealthy nationalism, where we identify with our own nation at the exclusion of others. That is not what we want anymore after what we have seen from Trump.

Things seem to be moving in this direction today. Leaders with nationalist leanings are more frequently taking center stage around the world, from the US, to Brazil, to India.

Because we tend to adopt a common position on a topic to signal that we are part of a group, just like football fans wear certain colors or have tattoos to show their tribal loyalty.

Even strong individuals who stand up to oppressive regimes typically have shared ideals and norms with other members of a resistance movement. Rarely humans function alone.

This tribalism can all feel very visceral and natural because, well, in a way, it is. It fires up the primal parts of our brain that evolved for such responses.

Other natural attitudes, such as compassion and consideration for others are also available. They can be suppressed in such circumstances.

This combination of nature and nurture shaping our attitudes and behavior is apparent in many human characteristics and unpicking some of these examples can help us see opportunities to steer the process.

Consider the tendency to become overweight in modern society. In premodern times, sugary and fatty foods were rare and valuable for humans. Now, they are everywhere.

A biological trait – the craving for sugary or fatty foods – which was adaptive in premodern times, has become detrimental and maladaptive.

Surely our modern cultures can protect us from these innate drives when they are unhealthy for ourselves and society?

After all this, we effectively suppress violent behavior in society through the way we bring up children, policing and the prison system.

Instead of acknowledging and protecting us from the innate drive to binge on unhealthy food, however, our modern cultures (in many countries at least) actually exacerbate that particular problem.

The result is billions of people – well over a quarter of the world's population – who are obese or have too much body weight, while another two billion suffer from micronutrient deficiencies.

When we understand how our "hardwired" urges interact with an unhelpful cultural context, we can begin to design positive interventions.

In the case of obesity, this might mean less marketing of junk food and altering the composition of manufactured food. We can also change our own behavior, for example laying down new routines and healthier eating habits.

But what about bigotry and xenophobia? Can't we simply design the right fixes for them? That may depend on how big the problems we face in future are. For example, growing ecological crises – climate change, pollution and biodiversity loss – may actually lead to more bigoted and xenophobic attitudes.

The cultural psychologist Michele Gelfand has shown how environmental shocks can cause societies to become "tighter" – meaning the tendency to be loyal to the "in-group" gets stronger.

These types of societies are more likely to elect authoritarian leaders and to show strong prejudices towards outsiders.

This has been observed under past ecological threats such as resource scarcity and disease outbreaks.

Under most climate change scenarios, we expect these threats, in particular extreme weather events and food insecurity, to only get worse. The same goes for the coronavirus pandemic. Many people hope such outbreaks can improve the world, but they could do exactly the opposite.

This enhanced loyalty to our local tribe is a defense mechanism that helped past human groups pull together and overcome hardship.

In response to global issues, becoming bigoted, xenophobic and reducing cooperation with other countries will only make the impacts on our own nations worse.

One of the scenarios was called "order from strength" and represented "a regionalized and fragmented world that is concerned with security and protection.

Countries see looking after their own interests as the best defense against economic insecurity, and the movement of goods, people, and information is strongly regulated and policed".

Later iterations of the scenario were called "fortified world" and describe a dystopian vision in which order is imposed through an authoritarian system of global apartheid with elites in protected enclaves and an impoverished majority outside.

On a larger scale, the rich "developed" countries, which are primarily responsible for climate change, do extraordinarily little to address the plight of the poorer countries.

There seems to be a lack of empathy, contempt and intolerance for others who were not fortunate enough to be born into "our" tribe. In response to an ecological catastrophe they have caused, rich countries simply discuss the best way to prevent the potential influx of migrants.

Fortunately, we can use rational thinking to develop strategies to overcome these attitudes. We can strengthen positive values, build trust and compassion, and reduce the distinction between our in-group and the "other".

An important first step is appreciating our connectedness to other people. We all evolved from the same bacteria-like ancestor, and right now we share more than 99% of our DNA with everyone else on the planet.

Our minds are closely connected through social networks, and the things we create are often the inevitable next step in a series of interdependent innovations.

Innovation is part of a great, interconnected creative human effort without respect for race or national boundaries.

Faced with overwhelming evidence from multiple scientific disciplines such as biology, psychology, neuroscience, one may even wonder whether we exist as discrete individuals, whether that sense of individuality is an illusion

We have evolved to believe that we are discrete individuals because it has provided survival benefits (such as memory formation and the ability to follow complex social interactions). But taken too far, egocentric individualism can prevent us from solving collective problems.

Beyond theory, practice is also necessary to literally rewire our brains – reinforcing the neural networks through which compassionate behavior arises. Outdoor community activities have been shown to increase our psychological connectedness to others, albeit right at this moment they are off-limits for those in lockdown. Similarly, meditation approaches alter neural networks in the brain and reduce our sense of isolated self-identity, instead promoting compassion towards others. Even computer games and books can be designed to increase empathy.

Finally, at the societal level, we need frank and open debate about environmental change and its current and future human impacts – crucially, how our attitudes and values can affect other lives and livelihoods.

We need public dialogue around climate-driven human migration and how we respond to that as a society, allowing us to mitigate the knee-jerk reaction of devaluing others.

Defusing a ticking ethical timebomb

Shame all those who stoke the flames of bigotry beneath it.

Instead, we can open ourselves up to a more expansive attitude of connectedness, empowering us to work together in cooperation with our fellow human kin.

It is possible to steer our cultures and rewire our brains so that xenophobia and bigotry all but disappear. Indeed, working collaboratively across borders to overcome the global challenges of the 21st Century relies upon us doing just that.

CPSIA information can be obtained
at www.ICGtesting.com
Printed in the USA
LVHW091416240121
677345LV00004B/778

9 789492 916969